Mirrors of the Soul

Seasons of Change, Volume One

Thalia Leigh Hope

This book is a work of fiction. Any references to historical events, people, or places are used fictitiously. Other names, characters, places, and events are products of the author's imagination, and any resemblance to actual events, places, or persons, living or dead, is entirely coincidental.

Copyright © 2025
All rights reserved, including the right to reproduce this book or any portions thereof in any form whatsoever.

For information, address:
thalialeighhope@gmail.com

To book Thalia Leigh Hope for any event,
contact thalialeighhope@gmail.com.

Cover photo: Thalia Leigh Hope
Cover and interior design: Book Puma Author Services
BookPumaEdit.com

ISBN: 979-8-218-85037-1

TABLE OF CONTENTS

Christlike Love	1	Saving Grace	50
Cry	2	Silent Grace	51
Repentance Plea	4	Father's Grace	53
Repentance Answer	5	Atoning Grace	54
Repentance Re-enforcement	6	Infinite Gift of Love	56
Worthy Strength	7	Unending Love	57
Silver Lining	8	Blessed Love	59
Climbing Higher	9	Transcending Love	60
Hold On	10	Searching	61
Holding On	11	Finding	62
Faith	13	Silent Whisperings	63
Growing Light	14	Loving Hands	64
My Light	15	Healer's Hand	65
The Light	16	On The Wind	67
Merciful Light	18	What I Can't See	68
Peaceful Light	20	Living Spark	69
His Light	22	Sparking Hope	70
Testimony	23	Childlike Eyes	71
Guide My Life Each Day	24	Give My All to You	73
Heartfelt Pleas	27	Breaking Chains	75
Christmas Gift	28	Sin	77
Earth's Heavenly King	30	Losing Ground	78
Matchless Gift	32	A Little Cry	79
Easter Gift	33	In My Need	80
Truthful Ministry	34	Temptation's Tricks	81
Gethsemane	38	Gold Refined	83
Godly Wisdom	39	Simply Truth	84
Tempest's Rage	40	Shining Truths	85
Christ Forgives	42	Piercing the Storm	87
Introspection	43	Beautiful Day	89
Sacrament Prayer	44	Unseen Trials	90
Merciful Lord	45	Fleeting Moments	91
Touching Faith	46	Letting Go	93
Trusting Faith	47	Spirit Freedom	95
Healing Faith	48	About the author	96

To my uncle, Benjamin, who has been patiently waiting for me to get on the ball and who has always believed in me.

To all my family and friends who have encouraged me in my love for poetry. I wouldn't have gotten this far without them.

To my Heavenly Father, who blessed me with the gift of words.

CHRISTLIKE LOVE

Patience, child you will see
Walk tall, a daughter of God
Things will become clear through me
Feet planted on gospel sod.

He sent his son here for you
On the cross he freely died.
In Gethsemane bled for you
Drops he spilt each time you cried.

Crown of thorns upon his head
Royal Daughter, loving friend,
Wanderers like you he led
Love is constant to the end.

Bitter cup shrank not to drink
Spear men pierced him in the side
You are worthless still you think?
Never was an easy ride.

Thy Christlike love from start to end
Redeemer of mine, save a place
Place in thy heart for loving friend
Returning there from a long race.

CRY

O Lord, Why am I such a fool?
My tears they fall, I cry a pool.
I bow my head in plea to thee
Then feel your arms encircle me.

Your arms hold me tight, warm embrace
I look up and see your gentle face.
I know you see. I know you care.
Why can't I always feel you there?

Am I so lost, so far from thee,
That even you can't bear to see?
I hold my head down in my arms,
Then you reach out, your spirit warms.

Your gentle voice whispers to me
My child, I am here for thee.
I am aware of all thy needs.
Thy weak soul I will surely feed.
Stay close to me, you will be strong,
Child never think you don't belong.
My dear, you will always be mine,
Keep on going, you will be fine.

I love thee, my child don't forget.
Please change what's wrong and no more fret.
Do what's right. You are always loved.
Come unto me, my child beloved.

Hold on tight, I am standing nigh,
You will be exalted on high.
I promised you I'd help you home.
My child, you are never alone.

I died for you upon the cross,
Your sins won't leave you at a loss.
For your sins, for you I was sent.
And you know that you must repent.

Repent and live. I will be here.
Please my child, don't you ever fear.
I love you, I will never leave.
Promise that unto me you'll cleave.

Thalia Leigh Hope

REPENTANCE PLEA

Father, How to draw near to thee,
When I feel far away from me?
Daughter of Thine, unworthy too.
Is there something for me to do?

My sins have driven me away
No matter how I longed to stay.
My Lord, My God, wilt thou forgive?
Help me to change the way I live.

The truth seems to have disappeared.
Why not live the way I was reared?
My valiant soul has gone from thee
so far away from even me.

The things I've done, the things I've seen
and all the places I've ever been.
Buttons I've pushed, the things I've said,
Sometimes I feel I'm better dead.
Help me, Lord, to see the light.

REPENTANCE ANSWER

Child, your sins are forgiven thee.
Take valiant stand, remember me.
I'll guide you: I will take your hand,
If for truth and right you stand.

I love thee, I'll never leave thee.
Stay close to me-Your guide I'll be.
Hold tight to truths you know are right.
I'll lead you home into the light.

I gave you life, your Lord am I.
With you I always will be nigh.
Thy Lord, the God shall ever be.
To you my child love comes from me.

Stay strong, Stay true, I am on your side.
Hang on tight for your troubled ride.
Please take a valiant stand for me.
Thy sins will be forgiven thee.

Thalia Leigh Hope

REPENTANCE REINFORCEMENT

Child, thy sins again are forgiven thee.
Take valiant stand. Still remember me.
Thou my Child will never be alone.
Take my hand and I will guide you home.

As you hold to what you know is right,
You know you'll more often see the light.
I know thee, Your weaknesses I see.
Soon your strengths they will become through me.

Again I love you and care for thee,
And still want you to return to me.
With great honor will be thy return,
If you have love and care for me in return.

Stand with valiant faith and head held high
Please remember, Heavens always nigh.
I will be with thee, forever near.
I will keep thee safe, my child dear.

Once more, thy sins are forgiven thee.
Keep thy valiant stand and soon you'll see
That I am far closer than you know.
Reach up, take my hand, your faith will show

WORTHY STRENGTH

You are tough, You are strong,
With me, you do belong.
Reach up your hand to me,
I'll give you strength to see.

Child, thee I'll always love.
With me you'll live above.
More worthy than you think
Do not let your self sink.

Hold tight to what is right.
You know you have a light.
Shine it for all to see
As you glorify me.

Though you have all your trials
Don't let them cramp your styles.
You're stronger than you know,
So keep your strength to show.

The path help all to see,
And they'll look up to thee.
Find your light, let it shine.
And Child, you will be mine.

SILVER LINING

A quiet light
A gentle song
It will go on.

Journeys begin,
Hope for a friend
Strong to the end.

Love one day lost,
Find it again.
Relief from pain.

Trials seem to end,
But they are not gone.
They do go on.

CLIMBING HIGHER

These feelings are too strong.
Will they ever belong?
They are so out of place,
There just isn't the space.

So much anger and hate.
I fear it is too late.
Can my life turn around
Or am I in the ground?

My happiness was gone,
Before my life went on.
I want to change my ways
And see some better days.

I need the help I get
I'm not perfected yet.
Turmoil in my life
Prepares me for the strife.

In my challenge I turn
for God and help. I yearn.
With him, I overcome
My true self, I become.

I can bask in his love
Then live with him above.
I'll return to him there,
And live with his care.

HOLD ON

The darkness surrounds,
The sun ne'er shines,
The evils within, around
Have now come forth.

Thou that hast gone astray
Must find somehow
A wat to in faithfulness stay
And never fall from steadfastness.

And when the light shines again,
Strive to keep the glow.
Keep the light growing within,
The light that thou hast grown.

The light shall then be strong and deep,
Many shall continue to help their light grow,
And the light strong and sure they shall keep,
And add to it forever as they go on.

Hold fast to the light,
Never let go,
Hold on with all thy might,
And thou in faithfulness shall stay.

HOLDING ON

Holding on with all my might,
Clinging to the rod of light.
Satan mocks my feeble strength
As I come to Thee in faith.

Thou wilt whisper peace to me
Giving hope I can be free.
In Thy arms Thee holds me close
And Thy Spirit to me flows.

Quietly Thou reaches out
To keep me safe through bout.
Gentle love wraps round me warm
At the sound of this alarm.

My daughter, again I'm here.
I won't let thee fall to fear.
Put thy trust in me alone
While thou livest far from home.

Cry to me in all thy need,
Live like me in word and deed.
Satan cannot bring thee down
If thou loves all around.

Temptation will come and go
But my mercy still will flow.
I will help thee through thy pain,
Thou wilt find thy strength again.

Thy weakness will become strong
When with me thou wilt belong.
Look to me in every thought,
Trust in me and doubt me not.

I know the strength in thy soul,
Faith in me will make you whole.
Trials come to help thee grow,
And my daughter, thou doth know.

Remember the truths ye find,
Study them in heart and mind.
Peace will come as ye move forth,
And you'll know thy Heav'nly worth.

FAITH

Walk by faith, do what's right
Standing strong in the light.
Light of Christ, love so pure
You'll find his grace is sure.

Faith so bright, in your heart
You'll find has taken part.
In your heart and your mind,
Feelings one of a kind.

Thalia Leigh Hope

GROWING LIGHT

Falling.
Falling fast.
Darkness enters-
Fading from the light.

Reaching.
Reaching out.
Looking to God-
And I fall again.

Mistakes.
Mistakes made.
Satan laughing-
Pulls my growing chains.

Tightly.
Tightly locked.
Pulling harder-
Clamping my chains shut.

Let go!
Let me out.
Crying "My Lord"-
Falling to my knees.

Touching.
Touching faith.
Feeling His arms-
Wrapping me with warmth.

Trusting.
Trusting Him.
Praying for help-
Learning He is near.

MY LIGHT

The Lord has always been my light
I'll follow him with all my might.
He is the everlasting Son
And He is the Anointed one.

He set us an example
That no one must trample.
We are the chosen ones
The Kings Daughters and his Sons.

Never said it would be easy,
He just said, "Come and follow me"
He'll gently hold us in his arms
And also keep us safe from harm.

He will always be there
And He will always core.
I now decline to say
How wrong I was one day.

I know we are here for a reason.
We must never fall for treason.
For He will always see us through.
But we must always remain true.

We must all be ready
For His coming, to see
Our Lord, Savior and Friend.
To live with him again.

He will forever be close by.
He's there wherever I cry.
So I must always do my best
And strive so hard to take the test.

THE LIGHT

He is the rising Son,
They light of the East.
The only Begotten One.
He loves to teach.

The Lord is the light
Light of the World.
Shadows removed from sight.
We can overcome our hurdles.

He opens his arms
find strength in his love.
Basking in his warmth
Return to him above.

He is always nigh
Never far away,
Gives us strength to try
Growing stronger by the day.

Faith in him increase,
Love of his will grow.
Life is light beneath
Letting your shine show.

You are his child.
Daughter of God
Once in awhile
Strayed from Gospel Sod.

He will help you come
Back into his arms
He'll help you come home
And stay in his warmth.

He loves you
So very much
And He needs you
To feel His touch.

He does long for you
Waits for your return.
He will fight for you
and help your fire burn.

You can keep his light
And shine it for all.
Your goal is in sight.
Heed unto his call.

His arms open wide,
He feels your pain.
and takes you aside.
Prayers are not in vain.

Thalia Leigh Hope

MERCIFUL LIGHT

In the silent, starry night
I was searching for a light-
Guides me from the rocky shoals,
Helping me to reach my goals.

Looking, searching high and low,
No idea of where to go.
Lost and stumbling in the dark,
Slowly straying from my mark.

Straining, reaching, I cry out,
Hoping someone hears my shout.
Falling, tumbling quickly down,
Farther from my promised crown.

Just before I hit the ground,
Comes a voice of softest sound.
"Hold, my Child, I am here.
And always have I been near.

Turn around and look to me,
And my light I'll give to Thee.
For thee I suffered on the cross
That gold may come from dullest dross.

I have come to help thee home,
Don't forget you're not alone.
For you I paid the highest price
When I was born to give my life.

I forgive you of your sins,
Go ye forth, hold high your chin,
Turn to me in deep duress
That I may relieve your stress.

Don't forget when times are swell
To turn to me then as well.
Thee my daughter I do love,
I'm waiting for you here above."

With this light my heart doth fill
And I live to do His will.
Looking forth to that great day
When in His glory I may stay.

Thalia Leigh Hope

PEACEFUL LIGHT

I'm standing strong,
I still belong.
Somewhere I've found
That peace surrounds.

My heart is full,
It feels the pull.
The heartstrings tug,
Receive a hug.

He leads the way,
He'll be my stay.
He helps me through,
Strength does renew.

Somehow I find
Some peace of mind.
Though I am down,
I cannot frown.

Light shines brighter,
Heart feels lighter.
Somehow, somewhere,
He will be there.

The beauty comes
Pain becomes numb.
God-given sign,
It's all in line.

Part of His plan,
Know that we can
Forward press on,
Pain will be gone.

I wait for Thee,
Please hear my plea.
Comfort I need,
Hear and give heed.

My heart be still,
Time enough to heal.
All will subside,
Go for the ride.

Thalia Leigh Hope

HIS LIGHT

I see the light coming near,
I have no reason to fear.
He will help me back to Him,
Give me strength through thick and thin.

As I stand up tall and strong
He tells me I do belong.
My heart fills and then takes strength,
For Him I'll take any length.

A gentle thought to my heart,
Says "Never from you I'll part.
Stay closely here next to Me,
Your gentle guide will I be."

Arms embrace and hold me tight,
Safe and warm; forever right.
His words fill my soul with joy,
Like a child with a new toy.

He'll now and forever be
My Lord God to comfort me.
His warmth starts to fill my soul,
I slowly crawl from my hole.

His light fills me, bright and pure-
I soon feel more strong and sure.
A whispered song; don't forget-
You're not quite perfected yet.

TESTIMONY

Do I know
In my heart
The things I think I know?

Do I actually have
A testimony-
Am I just going through the motions?

Have I overcome
The things that I've done?
Have I forgiven myself?

Who am I,
Daughter of God.
Become what I'm worth.

Can I do that,
Become what I want to be?
Will it ever happen?

I feel Him,
Calling to me
To him I must respond.

Take the old me
In my arms-forgive.
Come forward to who I am now.

It's tough to repent,
Find out the truth.
I know there's a purpose for me.

I promised in the Pre-existence
In order to keep what I promised,
I must learn to know.

Thalia Leigh Hope

GUIDE MY LIFE EACH DAY

Look-look towards me
See how others see.
A bright shining girl
Send rays to the world.

Smiling day by day
I hide from my ray
Withdraw the dark
Missing my own mark.

How to let them know
Through my words that flow?
With my trembling voice?
Do I have a choice?

Girl behind the mask
Poison from my flask.
Knife that draws so near
Lord my plea please hear.

Oh beckon angels!
Guide me from my shell.
Gently set on ground,
Walls come tumbling down.

Comfort, shelter, please
I am down on my knees.
Shelter from the storm,
Wrap round arms so warm.

Please my soul cries out,
Things to pray about.
Where's thy loving care,
Have I left thy lair?

In shame left the fold
Arms that gently hold.
Turning back to thee,
Now too late for me?

Straining hard in might
Searching for the light
Pain ripping my soul
Soon no longer whole.

Then come ray of light
Shining oh so bright.
Guide me to the path
All my Father hath.

He's leading me home,
I am not alone.
My Father is there,
Showers me with care.

Help me always know,
Thou art where I go.
Thou wilt lead me home.
Never was alone.

Thy sheltering arms
Gently keep me warm
Remind me of thee-
Thou art close to me.

In my heart abide,
Keep me from the tide.
I can change my ways
Going day by day.

I will not fall far
If I raise the bar.
Trust in Thee, My Lord
Daily live Thy word.

With Thy help I come,
Back to loving home,
Thou art waiting for me,
Hoping I will see.

Love for me grows strong,
Surely I belong.
Thou art pure and sweet,
Will save me from defeat.

(Chorus 1)   *(Chorus 2)*

The mask that hides me,   Masks have hidden me,
Girl the world sees.   Girl the Father sees
Lord to Thee I pray,   Lord to Thee I pray
Guide my life each day.   Hear my prayers each day.

HEARTFELT PLEAS

Help me now to find a way
Teach me all that I must say.
Help me learn to do his will.
His light in me instill.

Show me all that I must do.
Help me now to become new.
Angels round me help to show
Exactly how far I must go.

Here am I reaching to you.
Asking thee to pull me through.
To my knees I fall and pray,
Please help me to find the way.

Thou once drank the bitter cup.
And I ask thee to pull me up.
Falling fast and oh so far,
Help me now to raise the bar.

Pull me up and far away
From the pain I face each day.
Guide me back to thee from here,
When I follow, Thou art near.

Show me of the wondrous love
Sent to me from up above.
Wrap thy arms around, I pray.
Help me now to find the way.

Thalia Leigh Hope

CHRISTMAS GIFT

Silently He lay His head,
Angels round His manger bed.
Choirs singing thru the skies,
Praises sung to God on High.

Jesus Christ, Anointed One,
Mortal Reign is just begun.
Come to teach and life to give,
That all may return and live.

Mother Mary's gentle love,
Held close this gift from above.
She knew of His Godly worth,
Loved Him fierce right from His birth.

Angels praise and glory give
Holy Babe on earth to live.
Father bathed Him with His love,
Circling gently as a dove.

Shepherds came and left their flocks,
Saw the Lord in swaddling cloths.
The Lamb of God, Shepherd true,
Knew so young just what He'd do.

The wondrous story oft retold
Of frankincense, myrrh, and gold.
Wise men came and saw the Son,
God's Beloved, Atoning One.

His mission here to fulfill,
Preach his word and teach His will.
Loving gift for all mankind,
Gave His life to ease the bind.

Christmastime is meant for this,
Shows the way to Endless Bliss.
Don't forget this wondrous gift,
He is there, our souls to lift.

Silently He lay His head,
Angels round His manger bed.
Choirs singing thru the skies,
Praises sung to God on High.

Jesus Christ, Anointed One,
Mortal Reign had just begun.
Came to teach-and life He gave,
That all may return with faith.

Thalia Leigh Hope

EARTH'S HEAVENLY KING

The Holy child lay in His bed
With ox and lambs around His head.
Angels were gathered round the stall,
Singing praise to the Lord of all.

As Mary gazed upon His face
God's Spirit shone throughout the place.
Joseph stood near, by Mary's side,
Meekness cloaked the new father's pride.

While shepherds watched in nearby hills
An angel breaks their peaceful still.
Fear not, said he, Great joy I bring,
Glad tidings of Earth's Heavenly King.

For Christ is born in David's land;
In manger lain by Mary's hand.
Tenderly wrapped in swaddling clothes;
Joseph keeps watch in deep repose.

Heaven bursts forth angelic throng,
Glory to the King! Triumph's song.
Once still again the shepherds turned,
Let us go see of what we've learned.

Mirrors of the Soul

Wise men traveling from afar
Followed the shining glorious star.
To the stable they came with haste
To give the Lord their greatest praise.

Came the Kings to the manger fair,
To see the Father's One True Heir.
Brought they frankincense, myrrh, and gold,
All glorious wonders to behold.

Kings knelt to worship Him as King,
Who life and light to earth did bring.
Departed they the other way,
King Herod's jealous hand to stay.

We celebrate at Christmas time
This glorious King in every clime.
His the most perfect gift of love
Was sent to us from high above:

That we who dwell on earth below
Could always and forever know-
He is the way all may return
To home on High for which we yearn.

Thalia Leigh Hope

MATCHLESS GIFT

Here it's Christmastime again,
Tale of He our timeless friend.
Hear the Herald Angels sing,
Christ the Lord our Heav'nly King.

As He lay in gentle night,
He the Lord did bring us light.
The star shining high above
Led to Father's gift of love.

Throngs of Angels spread the word,
Born this night is Christ the Lord.
Shepherds came to worship Him
In the stable there within.

Herod sent the wise men there,
And they worshipped Him with care.
Oxen stood around His bed,
Knowing He the Lord, life bread.

Mary knelt in humble awe
At the beauty there she saw.
Joseph knew His Father's son,
Savior of the world to come.

This His precious gift of life
Given to the world of strife,
Now the perfect Christmas gift
Helps us all our souls to lift.

And now thru this Christmastime,
Let's remember of this rhyme
As we glory in His birth,
He the Savior of the earth.

EASTER GIFT

Step by step I follow Thee,
Learning how to become free.
Bit by Bit I come to know
What love for me Thou didst show.

When Thou died upon the cross,
Thou didst take with Thee my dross.
Whipped and beaten for my sins,
My whole soul for Thee to cleanse.

As we come to Easter Day,
Burdens at Thy feet I lay.
Thou didst rise for me again,
Thus canst Thou heal my pain.

In my sorrow, Thee I find,
Follow Thee in deed and mind.
I know Thou canst make me whole,
To the deepest of my soul.

In my darkest hour of need,
Thou didst take my hand and lead.
Kept me hidden from the knife,
Guiding me within my strife.

Leading me to safety there
In Thy loving, gentle care.
Thy arms wrap around me safe
As I follow Thee in faith.

Love that settles in my heart
As I strive to do my part.
In my changes Thou art near,
Teaching me to never fear.

Thalia Leigh Hope

TRUTHFUL MINISTRY

Silent hands were clasped in prayer
And an angel near was there.
There upon His bended knees,
Christ the Lord began His pleas.

Before our God, bowed His head,
Broke the chains and bonds of dead.
Kneeling, pleading, by the rock,
Satan trying hard to mock.

Suffering, with bleeding pores-
Only He could open doors.
Kneeling there unlocked the gate
For us to walk the path straight.

Taking all upon His back
Saved us from Serpent's attack.
Making all our burdens light,
Saving all within His sight.

Rescued sinners from our fate,
If we would unlock our gate,
Open up and let Him in,
Turn our backs on all our sin.

Silver passed through other hands,
Hands that led to where Christ stands,
Betrayed Christ because of greed-
He was passed-and done the deed.

Whipped and beaten, plaited thorns,
Clothing then was rent and torn.
Men then pierced Him in the side,
No one stemmed the lying tide.

Forced to carry beam through town,
Mocked and scorned as He fell down.
Nailed and hung upon the cross,
Sev'ral mourning for their loss.

Father, them their sins forgive,
Cried the Lord while still He lived.
They know not just what they do.
Then fulfilled was the plan true.

But not quite, for three days more
Laid He in the tomb before
The resurrection of life
Then gave God the glory rife.

Then Mary Magdolene wept
For the Lord who no more slept.
There inside the tomb was bare,
Where she knew He had lain there.

But then her joy was soon filled
Saw the Lord, her friend and shield,
Risen from His grave of stone,
Glory round about Him shone.

Thalia Leigh Hope

Dear woman, why dost thou weep?
Asked the Lord of His young sheep.
Tell me where you've taken Him,
And I'll take Him out again.

Mary Magdolene, my friend,
Here's your Savior to the end.
She turned and looked on His face
And saw her Lord in His grace.

And as He looked upon her
She found-trials she could endure.
At His feet she worshipped Him,
His Spirit warmed her within.

Bowing down upon her knees,
Christ the Lord answered her pleas.
And basking within His light,
Didn't want to leave His sight.

And now from this story we learn
That when help from God we yearn,
He is there to help us out
If we will remain devout.

If we yearn to feel His love
And believe that He's above,
Then the gift that paid the price
Helps us feel the glory rife.

He who paid the price for sin
Held the gate to let us in,
If we turn to Him in need
And repent in word and deed.

He promised to help us home,
And we know we're not alone.
This is why He came to earth
And He knew it from His birth.

This the wondrous gift of love
Was given us from above.
He who watches us by day
Longs to show us all the way.

So kneeling there at the rock,
Tempter's tools He tried to block.
Took our sins upon His back,
Giving us the strength we lack.

So begin to trust in Him
And the Spirit burns within.
He is the Begotten Son,
Jesus Christ-the Holy One.

Thalia Leigh Hope

GETHSEMANE

In a beautiful garden,
A place called Gethsemane,
He bled and He died for you,
Shared His Everlasting Light.

He poured His love out for you,
To gently help you come home.
He'll lead and guide you to Him,
Never worthless in his sight.

GODLY WISDOM

Teaching, preaching all His day,
Christ the Lord went on His way.
Twelve years old in temple sat,
Answered questions people hath.

Gave them knowledge, taught them truth
While even still in His youth.
They learned of the Father's joy,
Were astounded by the boy.

Thalia Leigh Hope

TEMPEST'S RAGE

Currents raging, tossing high,
And a blackness fills the sky.
In the boat Apostles call,
Maste, Master, Lord of all.

Carest Thou not if we die?
Why sleep Ye when storms are nigh?
Jesus rose and calmed the sea,
Why so little faith have ye?

Know ye not Divinity?
Though fearful, ye need not be.
Never will I let thee down,
Always will my love surround.

Like He calms the raging sea,
He calms the torrent in me.
While He mends my broken soul,
He alone can make me whole.

Whispering to help me heal,
He says these words, peace be still.
The anguish in me He calms,
Holding out His open palms.

Welcomes me with open arms,
Leading me back to His warmth.
My ship He'll guide to the dock,
At His firmly planted rock.

He enfolds me in a hug,
And I feel quite safe and snug

As He murmurs peace be still
While I listen to His will.

When I reach the Harbor's shore,
He then leads me to a door
Where He's waiting there beyond
To welcome me into His Throng.

Child, thee I'll not forsake
When in life ye make mistakes.
For thee I'll always be there-
I'll not fail; because I care.

Heav'n and Earth obey my will-
Here am I, so peace be still.
Fear not, for I am with thee.
I will calm thy troubled sea.

My friend, perish thou wilt not-
For courage and strength you've sought.
Thy prayers I do hear and feel,
So when I'm near, peace be still.

All I did I did for you,
Your pain and hurt all I knew.
Oft I've hoped for thee to feel
My gentle words, peace be still.

Feast upon my bread of life,
I will take thee through thy strife.
And from my cup, drink thy fill,
Then remember-peace, peace, be still.

Thalia Leigh Hope

CHRIST FORGIVES

They judged her for her sin,
To Christ they brought her in,
And told him in their pride
By law she won't abide.

We found her in her lust,
And this the law we trust
Says we must cast the rocks;
And tried the Lord to mock.

The Lord paid them no mind,
But they weren't satisfied.
Down in the sand He traced,
Then stood and them He faced.

If thou art perfect men,
With stones thou canst condemn.
On the ground still He drew,
And let His sentence brew.

Then all the men were gone,
He looked the woman on.
Hath no man condemned thee?
She looked around to see.

No Lord, was her reply.
And neither now do I.
Go thy way, live in light,
Strive to do all that's right.

INTROSPECTION

Lying on the dusty road,
There he was with wounds untold.
Angels watching as he lay,
While some went another way.

Stripped and wounded on the path,
They his beaters mocked and laughed,
Rudely left him nigh to death,
Strangers gave him prideful breadth.

In the silent wounded times
Of another's painful life,
Do I take the farther lane
Rather than the Spirit's flame?

As I trust my Father's love,
Do I follow Him above?
Will I go across the road,
Do I share with Him my gold?

He will help me when I fall,
He'll not leave me in the gall.
He will cover with His wing,
Strengthen me in everything.

Thalia Leigh Hope

SACRAMENT PRAYER

While this bread I humbly take,
Symbol of the bruises won,
As I still my sins forsake,
I remember Him God's son.

And this water now I drink,
Emblem of the blood He spilt;
From the evils now I shrink,
As I find the path He built.

When I take this Sacrament,
Peace will enter in my heart.
Leaning on the strength He lent,
Helping me to do my part.

As I listen to His will
And I try to gently hear,
Faith inside my soul instill,
Teaching me that He is near.

While my sins I now release,
And I think upon His love,
Here my faith He will increase
As I think on Him above.

As I think of how I've been
And repent of how I am,
His Spirit can enter in,
Son of God, Beloved Lamb.

MERCIFUL LORD

With just one plea,
He'll rescue me.
Turning to Him,
Healing begin.

He'll listen well,
My soul compel.
Holding me close,
Mercy He shows.

Thalia Leigh Hope

TOUCHING FAITH

His hands reach down to mine-
Guiding me line on line.
In faith to do His will,
Speaks in a voice that's still.

I must open my ears,
His words that I may hear.
With His strength, I can heal
If His Spirit I feel.

The woman in the road-
Knew the power He did hold.
In faith she touched His robe-
Asked He- Who touched my clothes?

Despite the crowd He knew-
One was healed through and through.
Back through the crowd He sought
The one to strength He'd brought.

As He turned, there He found
Her sitting on the ground.
Love then in His heart was filled
For she who had been healed.

I too can healed become,
When trust in Him I've won;
With my faith I am strong,
And numbered of His Throng.

Through His love I can find
A gentle peace of mind-
Turning to Him in need,
I can be healed indeed.

TRUSTING FAITH

As I pray to understand
Power of Thy guiding hand;
Reaching for a broader view,
Faith Thou helps me now renew.

In the dark I cannot see
Down the path Thou made for me.
I reach up to find Thee there,
Lonely burden Thou wilt share.

I know not what comes to pass,
At thy feet my sadness cast.
It's Thy will, not mine, that's done
As I come to know Thy Son.

Drawing near to Thee in need,
My wounded heart Thou wilt heed.
As I'm down upon my knees,
I trust Thee to hear my pleas.

Heart confused about this change,
Sort of feeling very strange.
Humbly asking for some hope
As I try with Thee to cope.

Since my path I do not know,
Follow with my faith to grow.
Now I find in humble awe,
My journey Thou surely saw.

Thalia Leigh Hope

HEALING FAITH

I can't pretend to know
As darkness seems to grow.
This world is coming fast,
Its evil shadows cast.
My faith is almost gone,
How can I still go on.

While trying to stay strong
The journey seems so long.
To reach the harbor safe,
I strive to find my faith.
The light will enter in
To help my fight with sin.

In time His light will spark
As I replace the dark.
He leads me back to joy
When faith in Him employ.
Sometimes it seems too hard,
But He will be my guard.

With me He will abide
As I drift through this ride.
My Shepherd He becomes
To lead the way back home.
He'll gently take my hand,
Lend strength to help me stand.

He shows me where to run
When I have come undone.
Gives me the peace I lack
When I have lost my path.
He'll teach me what to see
And all that I can be.

Then when I do believe
Unto Him I shall cleave.
When I on him will call
And then surrender all,
Darkness will fade away,
Within His arms I'll stay.

(Chorus)

Just believing on His name,
He who healed both blind and lame.
As I learn to call Him Lord,
He will strengthen me and more.

Thalia Leigh Hope

SAVING GRACE

Hands reach up to touch the sky,
And the Lord is standing nigh.
Heart of pain on bended knee,
The Lord reaches back to me.

His arms will stay open wide,
Helping through your troubled ride.
Standing outside He will knock
And wait for you to unlock.

Though trials will come your way,
He will guide you day by day.
He will not your souls forsake,
But He heals the burning ache.

When your sins are scarlet red,
Turn to Him the Lord-life bread.
Through Him your sins become wool,
His love then will pull you through.

Then holding on, feel His grace
Pull you through your struggling race.
And you'll feel His arms wrap round,
Keeping you warm, safe and sound.

Through His humble gift of love,
We each can return above.
He loves us and wants us home,
We must know we're not alone.

SILENT GRACE

Whispers softly through the night
Leads me back into the light.
My Father's voice, calling soft
Bringing me to higher lofts.

Loving child, I am here,
I will help thee thru thy fear.
I am always by thy side,
Guiding thru the serpent's lies.

As my Spirit touches thee,
Making thee what thou canst be
I will calm thy troubled heart
As I help thee do thy part.

Struggles in thy life will come,
Yet my child, no alone.
Come to me and find my grace,
I will help thee find thy place.

Child, thou art a budding queen,
Keep thy heart and spirit clean.
Turn to me in everything,
And thy spirit then can sing.

Adam fell that men might be,
And I help them come to me.
All thy sins the price is paid
Through the gift I loving gave.

Thalia Leigh Hope

I have seen the life thou left,
Daughter thou art surely blessed.
Thou art now becoming pure,
Turning to the rock that's sure.

Blessed child thou wilt see
All that thou canst one day be.
I am here to help thee home,
Let me lead when thou wilt roam.

Don't forget my gentle love
Sent to thee from up above.
I can stay here by thy side
If thou lets me fully guide.

FATHER'S GRACE

I try to find my way
In all I do and say.
This life is quite the task,
With all that Father asks.

While Satan tries to win,
It's hard to not give in.
The pressures of this life
Are full of toil and strife.

For every bitter taste,
The Lord will come with grace.
As His voice quiet speaks,
Through all our doubts to reach.

I hear Him whisper soft,
Trying to pierce my dross.
My daughter listen true,
Thou wilt know what to do.

Thy spirit is so strong,
Don't think thou won't belong.
I want to know thy heart,
Please strive to do thy part.

It's hard to see thy pain,
I'll lift thee up again.
Just turn to me in need,
Take my hand, let me lead.

My daughter thee I love,
I'm watching from above.
Just let me take thy load,
I'll lead thee on thy road.

Thalia Leigh Hope

ATONING GRACE

Gentle daughter, do not fear.
Know ye not I'm always near?
I'll not leave thee in the dark,
Thou hast not yet missed the mark.

Thru thy pain I quiet reach,
Listen to the words ye speak.
My gentle voice whispers soft
Thru the waves thou hast been tossed.

I hath sent the storms to thee,
Asking thee to trust in me.
I will be thy gentle stay
As I lead thee on thy way.

Thou hast yet a lot to come
On the path that leads thee home.
I will give thee strength to bear
All the burdens sent thee there.

Daughter thou art yet a saint,
And I hear thy soul's complaint.
Even those with mighty strength
Only run a little length.

I ask thee to do thy best,
Then I come to do the rest.
All I ask is for some faith,
Then I succor thee in grace.

As I come to lift thee up,
I will take thy bitter cup.
I can't take away thy pain,
But I'll give thee strength again.

I will bear thy burdens too
As with grace I pull thee through.
Peace will enter in thy heart
As ye strive to do thy part.

Satan's chains will harder pull,
Trying ye to falsely lull.
When the darkness closes in,
Turn to me in need therein.

With my strength ye can move on,
Sorrow, pain, and heartache gone.
My atonement was for all;
Every pain and every fall.

Ye can enter in my joy
But ye must my help employ.
I will help thee come back home,
Thou wilt reap what thou hast sown.

Thalia Leigh Hope

INFINITE GIFT OF LOVE

Child-thee thy sins forgiven,
To thee my love freely giv'n.
You know that for you I died-
And I know the tears you've cried.

I'm longing for you to see
The young woman you can be.
My hand reaches out for you,
Hoping you'll know what to do.

You know it won't be easy-
But you must know turn to me.
Angels circling you around-
Planting you on firmer ground.

Lifting you to higher heights,
Raising you with all their might.
Again stronger than you know-
Hold tight and don't you let go.

I'll lift you up, you'll be strong-
With me you'll always belong.
When you fall, I'll hold you close,
As I pull, my mercy shows.

UNENDING LOVE

As I'm learning once again
That thy love is without end,
Trying hard to turn to Thee,
Hear Thy voice calling to me.

Thy gentle words reach my soul,
Loving words to make me whole.
I forgive thee of thy sins
For I know thy heart within.

As you try to do thy best,
I will make up all the rest.
Thou must turn to me and feel
The light sent to help thee heal.

I am waiting here for you
As I teach thee what to do.
Lean on me in thy distress,
I will help thee find success.

Keep thy goals within thy sight,
Thou canst see what's wrong from right.
Use my Spirit as thy tool,
I will help thee win this duel.

Satan wants to win thy life,
As you've noticed in thy strife.
Do not let him take thee back,
I will be the strength thou lacks.

Thalia Leigh Hope

As thou struggles homeward bound,
I can lift thee from the ground.
Here I'm knocking at thy door,
I'm the harbor on the shore.

Reach for me, I'll take thy hand,
Lift thee up and help thee stand.
When life is rough hit thy knees,
I will listen to thy pleas.

I am waiting for thy cry,
I can give thee wings to fly.
Thou must give to me thy trust,
I'll help thee thy chains to crush.

I hope thou canst feel my love
As I'm watching here above.
Don't forget that I am here,
Thou won't ever need to fear.

BLESSED LOVE

In the darkness of thy gall,
Christ the Lord prevents the fall.
As thou turns to Him in need,
Follow Him in word and deed.

Through His gift of blessed love,
Thou wilt find He is above,
And He'll help thee come back home,
He won't leave thee on thy own.

As thy faith in Him increase,
He will from thy chains release.
As He whispers soft to thee,
Only I can make thee free.

Loving daughter I am here,
Once again thou need not fear.
Gentle words I'll quiet speak
As I try thy soul to reach.

Listen to my quiet words,
And you'll know I am thy Lord.
Follow me in all I ask,
Then gain all the Father hath.

Enter then into my joy,
After faith thou doth employ.
I will lead thee home on high,
Daughter I am always nigh.

Thalia Leigh Hope

TRANSCENDING LOVE

It's hard for me to see
The person I can be.
I have to let it go,
Perfect will I be? No.

But while I try my best,
My God will take the rest.
My Savior and my friend
Will guide me to the end.

My daughter I am here,
So be ye of good cheer.
It's what I'll always say,
I'll never run away.

Take heart and have some faith,
Thyself do not berate.
Good daughter be at peace,
Thy burdens I'll release.

Have patience and be strong,
Daughter ye do belong.
Although ye may feel weak,
My strength and comfort seek.

I love thee far beyond
An earthly, brittle bond.
I love thee with a love
Transcended from above.

My love will keep thee close
While mercy to thee flows.
Please let me keep thee safe,
And on thy heart engrave.

SEARCHING

I'm reaching my hand to you,
Calling you in all I do.
And still I tremble in fear,
Hoping, praying you are near.

Somewhere close I feel your love,
Show'ring me from up above.
In darkness I search for Thee,
Are you really there for me?

I close my eyes, bow my head-
Try to learn from all I've read.
Your Spirit comes, fills my soul,
And I'm longing to be whole.

Thalia Leigh Hope

FINDING

Child, child, I am here.
My Spirit comes, never fear.
I'll hold you in my embrace;
As I hold, you'll find your place.

I love you with all my heart,
Soon enough you'll play your part,
And through all, I'll keep you safe,
Hold you tight, guide through your faith.

Trust in me and do not doubt,
I'll never leave you without.
My child, come and follow me,
And I'll show you what I see.

SILENT WHISPERINGS

Within my heart Thy Spirit burns,
And for Thy love my Spirit yearns.
I long to feel Thy presence near,
To be one of Thy Chosen dear.

Here in my sin you try to reach,
My stubborn heart you want to breach.
There you stand, just beyond the wall-
To my inner light then you call;

My dearest child, oh my sweet.
I know these trials you can beat.
Child, child, little one.
Knoweth ye not the One True Son?

Must ye refuse to let Him in,
And let Him heal thy heart within?
For thee His life He freely gave,
Thy sins and hurt He meant to stave.

Open thy heart, my little one.
Please use the deed that has been done.
With love and light thy debt was paid,
And thy spirit has been remade.

Turn to Him in thy darkest need,
Then follow him in word and deed.
My little child, ye must be strong,
In my heart thou dost still belong.

Child don't forget thy Father's love,
Remember that we're here above.
To me thy spirit longs to turn,
Let it no more in sin now churn,
And glorious shall ye return.

Thalia Leigh Hope

LOVING HANDS

His gentle hands, holding me,
Guiding me the best to be.
Leading me to better things
And the joy His blessings bring.

He teaches with a gentle voice,
Barely heard above the noise.
Whispers softly, shows the way-
Gently prompting every day.

Freely shares His wondrous love,
Show'ring down from up above-
Felt in every drop of rain
Seen in flowers down the lane.

Lightly dropping new-felled snow,
He is with me ere I go,
Blessing me with beauty round,
In all things His love abounds.

HEALER'S HAND

The tempter's hand mocks my heart
As I strive to live my part
And turn to the greater good,
Doing everything I should.

Tempter knows the healing hand-
Enters in, the safety banned.
Tempter tries to overcome,
But the good's already won-

Now I see the evil lies
Thrown to hear my anguished cries.
Serpent thinks he owns my chains,
But they break against my strains-

Reaching God, He hears my hope
Then He throws a sturdy rope.
As I hold, He pulls me up-
He who drank the bitter cup.

My daughter I'm always here,
Pray for strength and don't you fear.
When you're weak then I am strong,
I'll keep you where you belong.

Trials come to show you've grown,
Showing you you're not alone.
Allow me to test your faith,
Lean on me, I'll be your strength.

Thalia Leigh Hope

I will lift you when you're weak,
If my strength you willing seek.
Call on me with all your might,
Know you're doing what is right.

I'll help you your burdens bear
When within my strength you share.
Hold on tight, you're doing fine,
Turn to me, your spirit shine.

I love you, my daughter dear,
By your side I'm always near.
Trust in me your gentle rock,
Tempter's hand will lesser mock.

ON THE WIND

Child who listens on the wind
In sight of God thou hast sinned.
Yet still art thou loved by me
Deeper than thine eye can see.

In the darkness of the night
You have tried to make things right.
Here I see thy broken soul,
How you long to be made whole.

Sins of thine I can forgive
If but for me thou wilt live.
Hard amends to make for sure,
Herein lies your only cure.

My gentle love through thee flows
Pulling all through highs and lows.
Live in my service you must,
Only then can thee I trust.

Do thy best and thee I'll help,
Don't rely upon thyself
To pick up when e'er thou falls,
For that's when to you I call.

My child list'ning on the wind,
Loving life you must begin.
Darkness of thy darkest night
Closing in will lead to light.

Thalia Leigh Hope

WHAT I CAN'T SEE

Gently on the cross He bows
Bearing all the Evil's scowls.
Thru the pain He humbly bears
All the strangers' mocks and stares.

All my sins He meekly bore,
Showing love forever more.
Oh how good and great Thou art
Gazing thru my bitter heart.

Pieces of my broken wounds,
Asking Thee to grant my boons,
Humbly turn my soul to Thee,
Giving me what I can't see.

Faith to learn and then to grow
Sharing all that I do know.
Peace to bind my broken heart,
Will to live the better part.

Strength to act the servant's role,
Shine like diamonds from the coal.
Breath to live a serving life,
Seeing those within their strife.

As I share Thy loving light,
May Thy Spirit shine so bright
So Thy face is seen through me
As from temptations I flee.

Grant me strength to do Thy will,
List'ning to the voice that's still.
He me love so all can see
Thy friend is the best to be.

LIVING SPARK

Child of the darkest night
Coming forth into the light.
In your early years of sleep
All you knew was but to weep.

Breath I spare that you may live
For the service you can give.
Now you're coming unto me,
Bigger pictures you can see.

Falling down upon your knees,
I can hear your echoed pleas.
Struggling through your deepest dark,
Shining forth your tiny spark.

In the middle of your fight,
Looking still for what is right.
Turn to me your guiding star,
Freely giving what you are.

Trusting me with all your cares,
I will take the pain you bear.
There you stand in humble need,
I will help you up indeed.

Thalia Leigh Hope

SPARKING HOPE

In the honesty of life,
You are in the lands of strife.
As you're searching to be whole
Let me in to fill your soul.

Spark of hope can be your light
While you try to make things right.
Step by step you make your way,
Take it slowly day by day.

Do not try to rush the end,
We can work through this my friend.
If you put your faith in me,
You will get where you can be.

Let me in to fill your heart,
While you strive to do your part.
You are worthy in my eyes,
I look past your many lies.

I see who you are inside,
Know you've had a troubled ride,
But I'm here to take your hand,
Get you on your feet to stand.

Let me be your living strength
As you go to any length
And become your very best,
To then in my presence rest.

CHILDLIKE EYES

Little One so meek and mild,
Thou that art the Holy Child.
Did you watch with gentle eyes
Stars and angels grace the skies?

Children now with eyes so pure
Know Thy love so strong and sure.
Young Isaiah, still so fresh,
Mother's arms inside he press.

Yet his eyes with stories to tell
Know the grace from whence he fell.
His tiny eyes shine so bright
As they reflect joyful light.

"Be as children. I implore,
Live with me forevermore"
Christ the Lord, Begotten One,
Fill my life with light of Sun.

Teach me now to be like child
And the Serpent be reviled.
Help me now to become strong,
Let me know that I belong.

Little children, oh so sweet,
Help me that time to repeat,
Show me how I may forgive
Trials which I've had to live.

Thalia Leigh Hope

Teach me through the youngest ones,
The evils therewith to shun,
And the blessings to behold
As I am refined to gold.

Angels come in many forms
To shelter us from the storms.
And as strange as it may seem,
Children, too, can redeem.

As angels disguised they come,
With buzzing spirits they hum
Of the light and life divine
From the Holy Spirit's shine.

With Angels' grace and mercy
Showing me the way to see,
Teaching me what I can be,
That I may return to Thee.

GIVE MY ALL TO YOU

I give my all to you
In everything I do.
I offer what I am
In anyway I can.

I found you in my slump,
Into your arms I jump.
You've gotten me this far
By being who you are.

I trust in you above,
And feel your gentle love.
Your arms wrap round me warm
Freeing me from the storm.

I turn to you in need,
Planting a little seed.
My seed begins to grow
When your light starts to show.

My faith in you increase
The sins inside to cease.
Giving my heart to you,
You show me what to do.

Thalia Leigh Hope

You hear my troubled pleas
As I fall to my knees.
You take me as I am
And I become your lamb.

You give your love to me,
Show me what I can be.
I cast my eyes up high
Hoping to search the skies-

To see your loving face
And your open embrace
That's calling me back home
Despite how far I've roamed.

BREAKING CHAINS

Chains inside begin to break,
Lets Him in to heal my ache.
When I kneel upon the ground
His arms wrap me tight around.

He has suffered all my pains
To help me break down the chains.
Yet as His heart reaches mine
He's teaching me line on line.

The soft presence of His love
Reaches me from high above.
Piercing me with tiny spark
Pulls me from my deepest dark.

Cleansing me from all my sin,
Burning in my soul within,
Healing me in every part,
Giving me a brand new start.

Gentle daughter, stand ye tall,
Thy sins are forgiven all.
I love thee with all I am-
Know my Son the Gentle Lamb.

Giving hope that you now feel,
He says these words; Peace be still.
Through Him thy sins be removed
If His gift you now behoove.

Thalia Leigh Hope

Selfless act of my dear Son,
Thy healing has now begun.
Here for you with every breath,
Loves you far beyond the death.

Gave His all in love for you,
Picks you up when e'er you fall.
If you turn to us in need
You'll find us in every deed.

We are here, your very strength,
We'll not fail in any length.
You belong with us in heart-
Do your best to do your part.

SIN

The walls are closing in,
I cannot find the way.
I'm trapped inside my sin,
And evil of the day.

Slip and fall, fading fast,
Ever farther I turn.
I turn to view my past
And think what can I learn?

How can I make this change
And be a brighter star?
I have myself estranged
From everything You are.

Now the farther I run
Is the deeper I fall.
Oh Everlasting Son,
To Thee I must now call.

Thalia Leigh Hope

LOSING GROUND

My strength is wearing thin,
The darkness closing in.
I cannot come to know
When I can't seem to grow.

I cannot find my route,
My heart is crying out.
I must continue on
And let Him break the bonds.

I cannot seem to breathe,
I'm trying to believe.
I still can see mistakes,
My soul I still berate.

My heart is still in two,
Fighting for what to do.
The goal is in my sight,
I'm looking for the light.

I want to make the change
And peace with Him arrange.
Temptations still amiss,
Yet now it comes to this.

I seem upon the fence,
So still my soul's entrenched.
I have to give my all,
But still too scared to fall.

A LITTLE CRY

Yet in my sin again,
I turn to Thee in pain.
Thy mercy flows through me
As I look up to Thee.

Thy whisper gently comes
While to Thy arms I run.
As ye stand strong in faith,
Thy struggles ye can face.

With trust in me above,
I'll send to thee my love.
The shelter of my wing
Will strength and comfort bring.

I go before thee, all
To strengthen in thy fall.
In mercy I reach out
To turn thee round about.

Remind thee of thy worth,
And of thy royal birth.
My daughter thou wilt find
Is always on my mind.

I'll lead my princess back
Through all who will attack.
And someday thou wilt be
In my home, safe with me.

Thalia Leigh Hope

IN MY NEED

To Thee in my need I turn
When my all is not enough.
Smallest darts begin to burn
As the going's getting tough.

To my knees I fall and pray
For the love to get me through
Every hour of each day-
Give me strength to follow You.

As I'm turning back to Thee,
Satan's chains he tighter pulls-
Fighting hard to stay with me,
My safety he falsely lulls.

Teaching me to hear his lies,
Calling me back to his lair.
But I know You hear my cries
And You'll keep me far from there.

As I turn to Thee in need
You my safety net will lock.
Take my hand and then You lead
To Your strong and rooted rock.

TEMPTATION'S TRICKS

I have to get a grip,
He's up to his old tricks.
I'm trying to stand strong,
Away from what is wrong.

Temptation has a hook,
I'm trying not to look.
I ask the Lord for strength
To hold unto my faith.

He wraps His arms around,
Lifts me to higher ground.
My daughter I am here,
There is no need to fear.

I'll calm thy troubled heart,
And strength to thee impart.
I know thy true intent,
My arm to thee I lend.

I send my mercy there
In answer to thy prayer.
I'll hold thee close to me,
And someday thou wilt see

My strength is in thy soul,
And thou hast been made whole.
The price I paid for you
Makes up what you can't do.

Thalia Leigh Hope

I'm always by thy side,
With thee I will abide.
Thy dross I turn to gold,
My grace will then unfold.

In thy search for the light,
I'll help thee do what's right.
And then will all be well
While close to thee I'll dwell.

GOLD REFINED

I give my sins to Thee
Upon my bended knee.
To make my dross to gold,
In turn to make me whole.

While fervently I pray,
The light to show the way.
I ask in humble need
With faith to plant the seed.

Thy arms envelop warm,
To shelter me from harm.
These words I gentle hear,
Come close my daughter dear.

I'm waiting thy return,
With longing I have yearned.
Thy sins forgiven all
Because on me you call.

I love you little one,
Thy work has just begun.
A tool within my hands
To shout to distant lands

The glory of the love
I'm sending from above.
My word shall come to pass
As all will see at last.

With faith you'll see the light,
And as you do what's right
I'll help you get back home,
A princess to become.

Thalia Leigh Hope

SIMPLY TRUTH

In light of the rising Son
With our faith we then are one.
Through our faith He'll gently heal
By the light and truth we feel.

Paid for us upon the cross,
Price that paid for all our loss.
Loving Son will come again,
Heal us from the plagues within.

Be like Children evermore,
Teach and love them I implore.
Show them how to come to me,
My example you will be.

All will see by word and deed
As my word you hear and heed.
Follow me and learn to love,
Return to me here above.

SHINING TRUTHS

At times it seems so dark,
I cannot find the spark
Or see the shining ray
Sent down to make my day.

I'm sitting on my sin
Have fallen once again.
Yet in this quiet spot
I try to find my thoughts.

My daughter I am here,
Though you cannot see me near.
I know thy troubled heart,
What role ye play a part.

Thy wants from me not hid,
Thy spirit lies amid
Temptations power high,
But I'll not let thee die.

For thee I have a path,
I'll guide thee with my staff.
Just turn to me in need
In all thy words and deeds.

My daughter thou I love,
Please trust in me above.
Mistakes thou still wilt make,
Life's not a piece of cake.

Thalia Leigh Hope

My child thy heart is pure,
Of that ye must be sure.
Thou art noble and true,
Reflect in all ye do.

Be ye perfect in me
Means so much more you see.
Be ye perfect in faith,
Hope, and love-thou art safe.

Temptations will not go,
But blessings from me flow.
It's not always easy
To come now unto me.

But as ye strive to learn,
And from the wrong to turn,
Ye shall be lifted up
By grace of bitter cup.

I gave my life for thee
In hopes you'll someday be
Back in my Kingdom's joy
As faith ye now employ.

Now be ye therefore strong-
How far ye've come along.
Stay close to what is right,
And thou wilt be my light.

PIERCING THE STORM

Gentle arms to hold me tight,
He will teach me what is right.
With loving voice He whispers soft
As He lifts me high aloft.

Angels' wings to beckon me,
Teaching me the way to be.
He will hold me in the storm,
Comfort comes in loving form.

Leading me to Him on high,
Giving me the strength to fly.
To the bitter heart comes peace
As the want to sin will cease.

While I look to Him above
Trying hard to feel His love,
His arms wrap around me safe
Teaching me to find my faith.

In my pain He quiet speaks,
Swiftly through my soul He streaks.
Child turn to me in prayer,
In thy life I long to share.

When you think to give it up,
Don't forget the bitter cup
I was sent to help you hold
As you are refined to gold.

Thalia Leigh Hope

I will be the strength you lack
As temptation you attack.
Let me in to fill the holes
Made in you by jagged shoals.

Don't forget I'm living still,
Helping you the ground to till.
As you're drawing close to here,
I will help you know I'm near.

BEAUTIFUL DAY

It's a beautiful day
With the brightest of rays.
Though the clouds may look dark,
There's the tiniest spark.

It's the spark we call hope,
Pulling up with a rope.
With Christ our guiding star,
We have nothing too hard.

He gives us strength to bear
The burdens we must wear.
And when to Him we call,
He's there to calm our fall.

He reaches out His hand
And pulls us up to stand.
He's gentle in the love
He's sending from above.

If we but follow Him,
The Spirit burns within.
He'll teach us what is right,
And then He shares His light.

Thalia Leigh Hope

UNSEEN TRIALS

Behind that little smile,
What is the unseen trial?
The pain that's locked away,
Will it be gone someday?

You might think you know her,
But she is so unsure.
She struggles with her faith,
She may be losing strength.

Behind her back you mock
With all your painful talk.
You do not understand
The shifting of her sands.

She stands on shallow ground,
Just trying not to drown.
Now you make fun of him
For being extra thin.

His dad has left the home,
They're striving on their own
To make their money meet,
So they can even eat.

The boy that's down the road
With scars and baggy clothes
Gets beaten ev'ry night,
And cannot see the light.

What right have you to judge
If you don't even budge
To fix your own mistakes
And then your sins forsake?

FLEETING MOMENTS

It slips away so fast,
Life's fleeting moments passed.
A mother gone at three,
The dad he needn't be.

Our friends that come and go,
The lover's flame burned low.
A prayer is in my heart
For each and every part.

The time we have is short-
We all will soon report
To Father's home on high,
So make the most we try.

In sickness, health, and joy,
It's faith we must employ.
The Highest Love knows best,
He puts us to this test.

Yet if we do stay strong,
We sound redeeming song.
No matter what the end,
We find a loving friend

If to our God we turn
And find what we must learn.
The Father of our kind
Does gently us remind

Thalia Leigh Hope

That in His courts above
We're with the ones we love.
Yet we must be His light
And strive to do the right.

This life does not just quit,
I know this every whit.
The veil is very thin,
I've felt the souls therein.

They're waiting for the time
That all the bells will chime,
And each of us be there
With all the ones that care.

Our Father takes the sting,
He helps with everything
As we come close to Him
And find the joy within.

LETTING GO

Anger, hurt, frustration too;
God on high, please pull me through.
Standing here on solid ground
And trying hard not to drown.

Bitter taste of all these years,
Now I struggle through the tears.
All the feelings I have stuffed,
Is it time to say enough?

Am I willing now to find
Darkest corners of my mind?
As I try to find my voice,
Spirit whispers of my choice-

Live in darkness all thy life,
Or find the way through this strife.
The choice is now up to thee,
Hold thy chains or become free.

Daughter don't forget I'm here,
I can sense that thou doth fear.
Don't forget my loving arms,
I can keep thee from thy harm.

This too for thee I have done,
And this battle can be won.
I can give thee strength to try,
And I'll give thee wings to fly.

Thalia Leigh Hope

In thy sorrow I will lead,
Turn to me in all thy need.
All this anger, hurt and pain
Is for thy good, for thy gain.

The time has come here at last
To heal thy pain from the past.
Know I will not let thee down,
I will be there all around.

Trust in me and feel my love,
I am guiding from above,
I was never gone away-
I Am always here to stay.

Show thy strength and lift thy head,
Give to me thy doubt and dread.
I will take thy wounds all hid
And be there, thy troubles rid.

SPIRIT FREEDOM

I may not understand
Thy gentle guiding hand,
Yet I know the Spirit
Thou teaches me to get.

I turn my heart to Thee,
Thou lets me now be free.
The anger I will hide
His Spirit can't abide.

What right have I to judge?
I walk in my own sludge.
My heart now needs be pure,
I'm trusting in the sure.

I know I'm doing wrong
Not helping her be strong.
His love I can't withhold,
So let Him take this load.

He'll teach me what is right
As He doth shine His light.
I hope I can be true
In all I need to do.

Thalia Leigh Hope

ABOUT THE AUTHOR

Thalia Leigh Hope was Utah born and raised. She has loved to write as long as she can remember. In junior high, she discovered word play in the form of poetry and automatically fell in love with it.

As a lifelong member of the Church of Jesus Christ of Latter Day Saints, the gospel is a deeply rooted part of her life.

When she's not writing, she's working hard and studying to be a professional editor.

www.ingramcontent.com/pod-product-compliance
Lightning Source LLC
Chambersburg PA
CBHW020309010526
44107CB00001B/37